W9-AOC-726

# A CONTINENT OF CREATURES

# The Animals of
# EUROPE

Tamra B. Orr

PURPLE TOAD
PUBLISHING

Europe is made up of many countries. The largest is Russia.

EUROPE

Russia

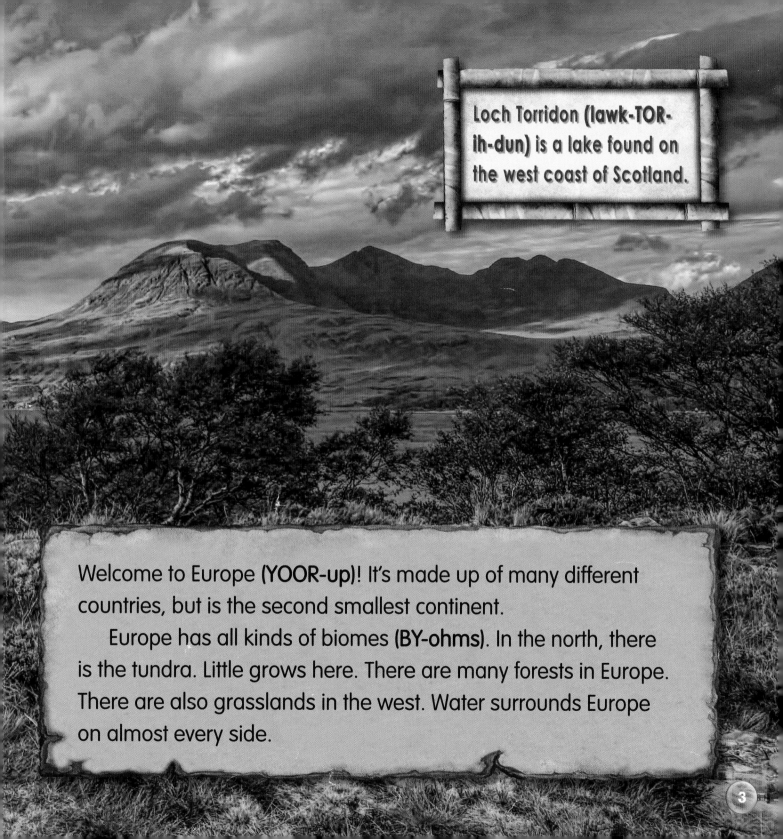

Loch Torridon (lawk-TOR-ih-dun) is a lake found on the west coast of Scotland.

Welcome to Europe (YOOR-up)! It's made up of many different countries, but is the second smallest continent.

Europe has all kinds of biomes (BY-ohms). In the north, there is the tundra. Little grows here. There are many forests in Europe. There are also grasslands in the west. Water surrounds Europe on almost every side.

We all know the story about Little Red Riding Hood and the hungry wolf. Did you know that the wolf was based on the European Gray wolf?

Gray wolves often live together in packs. Howling is their way of speaking to each other. When food becomes hard to find, they look for something to eat in nearby villages and houses.

No two reindeer antlers
are the same.

Europe is also home to the reindeer. In winter time, they live within the forests of Russia and Greenland. In the spring, they go back to the treeless arctic tundra. They are the only deer in which both males and females have antlers.

Wolverines can climb trees with their long claws.

Wolverines (WOOL-ver-eenz) are small and fierce fighters that live across Europe. They have claws, powerful jaws, and sharp teeth. They can smell food buried under 20 feet of snow.

The Fallow deer's white spots are bright during summer, but fade away in the winter.

Fallow deer are spread throughout Europe in places like England and Scotland. They love open and grassy areas.

Red foxes usually
hunt at night.

Red foxes live in the forests and farmlands of Europe. They mostly
sleep during the day wrapped in their bushy tails. At night they use
their senses to hunt for food.

Mink like fish but will also eat frogs, crabs, and even insects.

Found near some of Europe's rivers is the European mink. Its webbed feet make it a fast swimmer as it searches for tasty fish.

Badgers have very strong claws for digging in the ground.

Marbled polecats are usually more than a foot long with a very long tail.

The European badger (BAD-jer) and marbled polecat (POHL-cat) live in the grasslands and Europe's dry areas. Both live on a diet of frogs, birds, and lizards.

The sound of the cuckoo in Europe means it's spring.

The common cuckoo (KOO-koo) gets its name from the call the male bird makes. Cuckoos lay eggs in the nests of other birds. Mothers then go back and check on their babies after they hatch.

When several goldfinches gather together they are called a "charm."

The colorful European goldfinch eats thistle blossoms with their sharp, pointed beaks. They also eat seeds and insects. These birds can often be seen in gardens and parks.

The brown bear is the national animal of several countries in Europe. They live in a den, a hole dug in the ground or the base of a tree.

The European adder has a dark zigzag pattern on its back.

The common European Adder (ADD-er), or viper (VY-per), is the only poisonous snake in England. Males fight each other by doing "the dance of the adder." The two snakes lift themselves straight up and begin to push into each other.

A single bite from this spider can be deadly.

During the summer, people in Moscow, Russia know to watch out for the European black widow spider, one of the most dangerous spiders on earth.

The Wels catfish can come out of the water and grab ducks, frogs, and rats to eat.

Europe's lakes and rivers are home to the wels catfish. It can grow as long as 16 feet and weigh as much as a horse! It has a flat head and a wide mouth. It usually eats fish.

Lynx use their special coloring to hide. The fur on their ears helps them hear their prey.

The wild boar starts out with light fur, but, when full-grown, will either be dark brown or black.

Europe is a small continent. But it is full of amazing creatures in the air, on the ground, and in the water.

## FURTHER READING

### Books

Allgor, Marie. *Endangered Animals of Europe.* Powerkids Press, 2011.

Jackson, Tom. *The Illustrated Encyclopedia of Animals of Africa, Britain and Europe.* Lorenz Books, 2008.

Sherwood, Sandra. *Animals in Europe—Enjoy and Learn about Your World.* Amazon Digital Services, 2012.

Spilsbury, Richard. *Animals in Danger in Europe.* Heinemann, 2013.

### Web Sites

Details and fact sheets of Europe's endangered animals at Kids' Planet's

http://www.kidsplanet.org/factsheets/map.html

Printable images about European animals at Enchanted Learning's

http://www.enchantedlearning.com/coloring/europe.shtml

World Wildlife Fund's Europe Fact Files

http://gowild.wwf.org.uk/regions/europe-fact-files

**biome** (BY-ohm)—A community of animals and plants living together in a specific climate.

**continent** (KON-teh-nent)—One of the seven large land masses of the Earth.

**hibernate** (HY-bur-nayt)—To sleep and stay inside during the winter months.

**tundra** (TON-druh)—a plain with very little plant life having a permanently frozen layer below the surface.

**viper** (VY-purr)—A type of dangerous snake.

**PHOTO CREDITS:** pp. 1, 7, 14—Tambako the Jaguar; p. 2—Oliver Clarke; p. 6—Alexander Buisse; p. 8—Steve Slater; p. 10—Immortel, Kalerna, Marie Hale; p.12—Vogelartinfo, Andreas Trepte; p. 14—Katanski, Andieaze; p. 16—Andre Daniel, Mihalca, Highlandtiercel; p. 18—Cameraist, Dieter Florian; p. 20—Bernard Landgraf, Sander van der Wel. All other photos—Public Domain. Every measure has been taken to find all copyright holders of material used in this book. In the event any mistakes or omissions have happened within, attempts to correct them will be made in future editions of the book.

# INDEX

Copyright © 2017 by Purple Toad Publishing, Inc. All rights reserved. No part of this book may be reproduced without written permission from the publisher. Printed and bound in the United States of America.

Printing   1        2        3        4        5        6        7        8        9

The Animals of Africa
The Animals of Antarctica
The Animals of Asia
The Animals of Australia
The Animals of Europe
The Animals of North America
The Animals of South America

ABOUT THE AUTHOR: Tamra Orr is the author of hundreds of books for readers of all ages. She loves the chance to learn about faraway lands and to find out what it is like to live there—all from the comfort of her work desk. Orr is a graduate of Ball State University, and is the mother of four. She lives in the Pacific Northwest and goes camping whenever she gets the chance.

**Publisher's Cataloging-in-Publication Data**
Orr, Tamra.
   Europe / written by Tamra Orr.
      p. cm.
Includes bibliographic references, glossary, and index.
ISBN 9781624692680
1. Animals—Europe—Juvenile literature. I. Series: A continent of creatures.
   QL253 2017
   591.94

eBook ISBN: 9781624692697

Library of Congress Control Number: 2016937185

PURPLE TOAD
PUBLISHING